Usborne First Experiences
Going to the Dentist

Anne Civardi

Illustrated by Stephen Cartwright

Edited by Michelle Bates
Cover design by Neil Francis

There is a little yellow duck hiding on every double page. Can you find it?

This is the Judd family.

Mr. Judd

Mrs. Judd

Jake Judd

Jessie Judd

Jasper

Jake and Jessie need to have a check-up with their dentist.
Mr. Judd phones to make an appointment.

A few days later, they go to see the dentist.

Mrs. Judd takes Jake and Jessie in her car. Jasper goes too, but he won't be allowed to go in with them.

The dentist is very busy.

There are lots of people waiting to see him. Jake and Jessie play in the waiting room until it is their turn.

Jake and Jessie meet the dental nurse.

She calls them in to see the dentist. She is going to help with Jake and Jessie's check-up.

"Hello Jake, hello Jessie," says the dentist.

"Hello," say Jake and Jessie. The dentist says that Mrs. Judd can come in and watch.

Jessie goes first.

The dental nurse puts a bib around Jessie's neck.
Then Jessie sits in a special chair that can go up and down.

Jessie has her teeth checked.

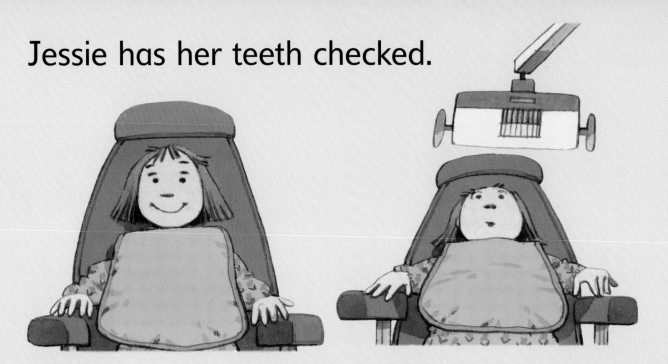

There is a spotlight above Jessie which shines into her mouth.

The dentist wears special gloves and a mask over his nose and mouth. He puts the chair back before he checks Jessie's teeth.

Jessie opens her mouth wide. He uses a mirror to see inside.

The dentist looks at each of Jessie's teeth. The dental nurse writes down notes about them.

The dentist has finished with Jessie.

He is very pleased with her. Jessie has no holes in her teeth. Now she can rinse out her mouth.

Now it is Jake's turn.

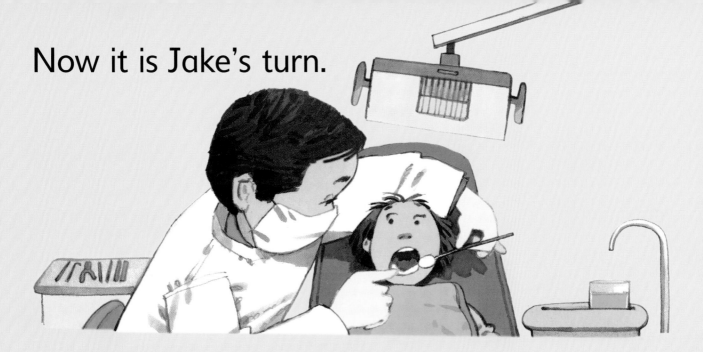

When the dentist checks Jake's teeth he finds a small hole in one of them. This means that Jake needs to have a filling.

The dentist decides that Jake's tooth should be numbed. He rubs on some gum paste and gives him an injection.

Jake has a filling.

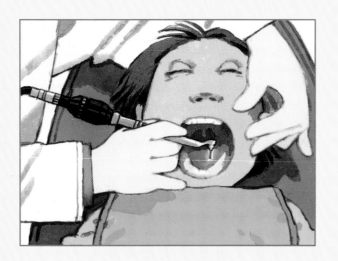 

The dentist drills away the bad part of Jake's tooth. The dental nurse keeps it dry with a suction pipe.

Then she mixes a special paste to put into the hole. It is shiny and white.

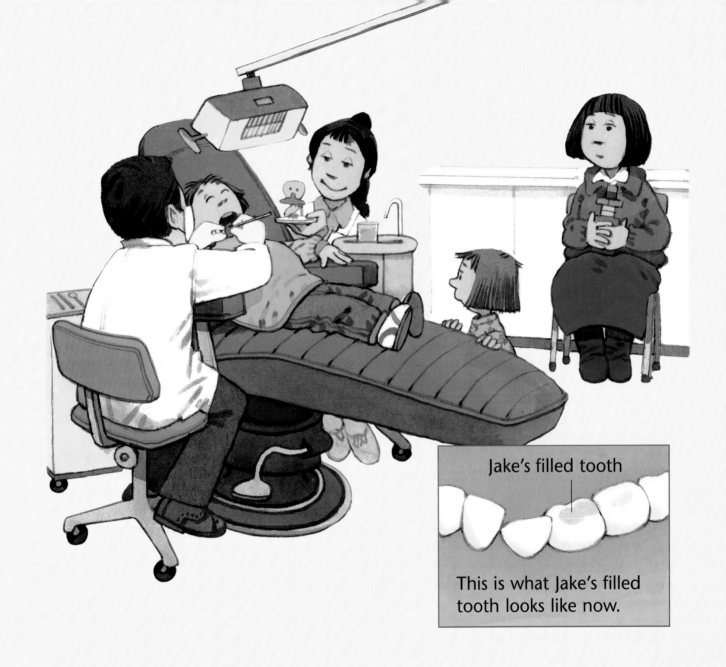

Jake's filled tooth

This is what Jake's filled tooth looks like now.

The dentist presses the paste into the clean hole. Now Jake will not get a toothache.

The children learn how to look after their teeth.

Unhealthy teeth and gums look like this.

Healthy teeth and gums look like this.

The dentist shows them what will happen if they don't take care of their teeth properly.

Eat more of these

Eat less of these

He says they should be careful what they eat and drink because sugar and sweet foods and drinks are bad for teeth.

The dental nurse shows them how to brush their teeth really well. This gets rid of old food which can cause holes.

Jake and Jessie must brush their teeth twice a day with fluoride toothpaste to keep them clean and healthy.

Jake and Jessie go home.

On their way out, Mrs. Judd makes an appointment to see the dentist for another check-up after six months.

This edition published in 2005 by Usborne Publishing Ltd, Usborne House, 83-85 Saffron Hill, London EC1N 8RT, England.
Copyright © 2005, 1992 Usborne Publishing Ltd. www.usborne.com
First published in America in 2005. UE
The name Usborne and the devices 🔅 🌐 are Trade Marks of Usborne Publishing Ltd.